Craft It Up
Christmas
Around the World

Craft It Up
Christmas
Around the World

35 FUN CRAFT PROJECTS
INSPIRED BY TRAVELING ADVENTURES

LIBBY ABADEE
AND CATH ARMSTRONG

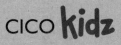

From Libby:
For my parents, Pat and Jon, for my sisters, Jane and Susan, and for Phil and our beautiful children, Angus, India, Jack, Gracie, and Emily.

From Cath:
For Ray and my children, Caitlin, Nicholas, and Marcus. Thank you for your support, patience, and most of all your laughter and love, which makes everything worthwhile.

Published in 2014 by CICO Kidz
An imprint of Ryland Peters & Small
519 Broadway, 5th Floor, New York NY10012
20–21 Jockey's Fields, London WC1R 4BW
www.rylandpeters.com

10 9 8 7 6 5 4 3 2 1

A CIP catalog record for this book is available from the Library of Congress and the British Library.

ISBN: 978-1-78249-156-9

Printed in China

Editor: Clare Sayer
Designer: Emily Breen
Photographer: Cath Armstrong
Templates: Stephen Dew

Contents

Introduction

Christmas is a time of year filled with nostalgia, sweet childhood memories, and special holiday festivities with family and friends. It is full of iconic imagery and wherever you live in the world, be it hot or cold, these images have a comforting similarity. From Santa to sleigh bells, stockings to snowballs and Christmas trees, we all recognize the same images at Christmas.

With our big families filled with children, we adore Christmas and the traditions surrounding it. Cath has experienced Christmas all over the world as well as back home in Australia, where it's the time to throw a shrimp or two on the barbecue! Libby grew up with white Christmasses in England, and a much more traditional idea of what Christmas should look like. Now she lives in the opposite hemisphere, she still hangs snowball ornaments on her tree and cooks a hot lunch in the summer sun!

In countries all over the world, Christmas is a holiday that brings people together. A chance to forge new memories and enjoy the company of family and friends. This book will show you how to make some new memories, whilst perhaps reminiscing about old ones. You'll sit down with your friends and family and make precious heirlooms that you'll enjoy taking out of the Christmas box year after year. Or you'll create a very special present to give away.

NORTH AMERICA

On your journey through our book we hope you'll learn that while we celebrate some things the same way, there are plenty of differences across the world. We've turned Christmas ideas from 35 countries into beautiful and unique crafts for you to make.

Discover when the ice rink was installed at the Rockefeller Center, and for what purpose, as you make a pretty Rockefeller Ice Queen (page 30). Learn how South American countries celebrate with nativity scenes as you make a tiny Matchbox Manger (page 34). Or discover the real spirit of Christmas with the Pay it Forward Advent Calendar (page 70).

We hope that you love this book and the beautiful crafts you'll learn how to make. We're sure you'll make some wonderful new memories.

Enjoy!

Cath & Libby

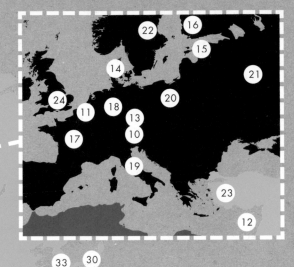

ASIA

AFRICA

OCEANIA

Map of the World

Chapter 1
The Americas

The Americas have a strong tradition of celebrating Christmas. The Christmas Tree at the Rockefeller Center in New York dates back to 1936! Why not try making a Rockefeller Ice Queen to celebrate your Christmas, or make a tiny Matchbox Manger, inspired by the nativity scenes of Uruguay?

"I'm Dreaming of a White Christmas" Snowflakes

ARGENTINA

These snowflakes need just a few simple materials, but when they catch the light, they are breathtaking! Try adding multifaceted crystal beads for extra sparkle and shimmer!

YOU WILL NEED
(FOR 1 SNOWFLAKE)

3 white or silver pipe cleaners or chenille stems

A selection of white beads, pearls, and crystal beads

White glue (PVA)

Clear nylon thread

1. Take three pipe cleaners and twist them together several times in the middle to make a star.

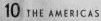

fun fact

In Argentina there is a strong European influence at Christmas time—although the weather is warm at Christmas, Argentinians use cotton balls on their Christmas trees to resemble snow.

2. Start threading beads onto each pipe cleaner and push as far up the stems as you can. Repeat until each stem is full.

3. Dab some white glue on the end of each pipe cleaner to hold the last bead in place.

4. Tie a piece of nylon thread to the end of one of the stems and cut as long as you like for hanging.

Chalk It Up Place Markers

BRAZIL

We've used sticky back chalkboard plastic for this project. It can transform smaller items quickly and cheaply. You could try adding it to gift tags or note books for gorgeous, personalized presents!

Megan

YOU WILL NEED
(FOR 1 PLACE MARKER)

MDF coaster

Self-adhesive chalkboard vinyl (alternatively use chalkboard paint and a paintbrush)

Dowel, about 6in (15cm) long

Strong glue or hot glue gun

Mini milk bottle

Festive candies

Chalk

1. Trace around the coaster onto the back of the self-adhesive chalkboard vinyl and cut out. If you are using chalkboard paint, paint one side of the coaster and allow to dry.

John

Marie

Anne

Lucas

Julia

2. Stick the chalkboard circle onto the coaster (you can skip this step if you are using chalkboard paint). Flip over and glue the end of the dowel onto the back of the coaster, using strong glue or a hot glue gun (ask an adult to help you). Allow to dry.

3. Pour some candies into the milk bottle and then stand the dowel in the bottle. Write your guest's name on the circle with chalk!

fun fact

Did you know that the Brazilian Christmas Feast is eaten on Christmas Eve? Called "Ceia de Natal," it is a traditional turkey dinner.

"Put Your Foot In It" Snowman Boot

CANADA

You don't need expensive fabric paints for this canvas boot project. Or fancy brushes. You won't be washing these boots so acrylic paint is suitable and durable. If the snowman starts to look less than crisp, just add another layer of paint to freshen him up!

YOU WILL NEED

Canvas "high-top" sneakers

Q-tips (cotton buds)

Acrylic paint in white, green, orange, red, and black

Permanent black marker pen

Hot glue gun or strong glue

Small round silver diamantés

1. Dip a Q-tip in some white paint and paint on dots to create the shape of your snowman. You may need to build up a couple of layers to get the color you want. Allow to dry.

2. Using the same painting technique, dot some white snowballs around the snowman's head. Add a hat, carrot, and scarf; we've used green, orange, and red, but you can choose your own colors. Allow to dry.

3. Add the eyes with a permanent marker pen. Ask an adult to help you use a hot glue gun to glue diamantés onto some of your snowballs. We glued them on randomly but you could use diamantés on every snowball for more bling!

Sweetness and Light Centerpiece

COLOMBIA

Make a beautiful centerpiece for the Christmas dining table! Felt is a great material to work with as it's relatively cheap to buy, it doesn't fray, and it keeps its strong color really well.

YOU WILL NEED

Small leaf template on page 125

12 x 9in (30 x 23cm) dark green felt

Scissors

Green embroidery floss (thread) and needle

12 x 4in (30 x 10cm) pale green felt

Hot glue gun

12 x 7in (30 x18cm) red felt

A red button

12 x 4in (30 x 10cm) purple-red felt

Pinking shears

12 x 7in (30 x 18cm) gray felt

1 cork mat, approx 7in (18cm) in diameter

A red pillar candle

MAKING THE HOLLY LEAVES

1. Using the template on page 125, cut four leaves from the dark green felt.

MAKING THE BASIC FLOWER

1. Cut the pale green felt in half lengthwise.

2. Cut slits about 1½in (4cm) long all along one long edge of the felt strip.

2. Sew a line of running stitch in green embroidery floss up the center of each leaf. Knot the thread at both ends and trim.

3. Roll the felt up along the length and ask an adult to help you use hot glue to hold it together. Repeat to make a second pale green flower.

4. Cut a strip of red felt 12 x 2in (30 x 5cm) and repeat steps 2–3 to make a red flower. Ask an adult to help you use a hot glue gun to glue the button to the center of the flower.

MAKING THE LOOPED FLOWER

1. Ask an adult to help you use a hot glue gun along the long edge of the purple-red felt and then fold it in half lengthwise and stick it together.

2. Use pinking shears to cut slits about 1½in (4cm) long down one long edge of the strip, starting at the folded edge.

3. Roll up the felt along the length and glue as you did for step 3 of the basic flower.

4. Cut the remaining strip of red felt in half lengthwise to create two strips approximately 12 x 2½in (30 x 6cm). Repeat steps 1–3 above to make two smaller looped flowers, using regular scissors instead of pinking shears.

MAKING THE ACORN

1. Cut a piece of gray felt that is 12in (30cm) long, 2½in (6cm) wide at one end and ⅝in (1.5cm) wide at the other end. You should have a long tapered piece.

2. Use scissors to scallop along the tapered edge.

3. Ask an adult to help you use a hot glue gun to glue along the long straight edge. Roll up, starting at the wider end until you have an "acorn" shape. Repeat steps 1–3 to make three more acorns.

ASSEMBLING THE CENTERPIECE

1. Arrange your leaves, flowers, and acorns around the cork mat and glue, remembering to leave enough space for your candle. Make sure you use a candle that is taller than your display and never leave a burning candle unattended.

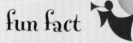

fun fact

The unofficial start to Christmas, or Navidad as Colombians call it, starts on December 7th. This day is widely known as El Día de las Velitas—"the day of the candles." Colombians light candles inside and out.

Jingle Bell Bracelet

CUBA

From the jingle of sleigh bells to the loud peals of church bells, everything feels Christmassy when you hear the sweet sound of bells ringing. This project will keep you jingling through December and beyond!

YOU WILL NEED

Embroidery needle with eye large enough to accommodate the thread

10in (25cm) stretchy nylon jewelry thread

10 felt balls, each ¾in (2cm) in diameter

10 tiny bells, each ⅜in (1cm) in diameter

Scissors

1. Thread the needle with the nylon jewelry thread.

2. Start threading felt balls and bells onto the thread, alternating them as you go. We used 10 of each for teen wrists but you might want to use more or less.

3. Tie the ends together and trim any excess thread.

fun fact

At midnight on Christmas Eve, church bells are rung across the capital city of Havana as Cubans attend midnight mass to welcome in Christmas Day.

Santa's Poinsettia Sack

MEXICO

Once you've mastered the iron-on appliqué technique used in this project, you'll be able to design your own t-shirts and start customizing clothes and household textiles. It's brilliant for using up little scraps of fabric.

YOU WILL NEED

Pillowcase (we used a bright red one)

Pins

Sewing machine (optional)

Needle and matching sewing thread

Safety pin

2¼yd (2m) cord

Flower cookie cutters in a few sizes or templates on page 123

Pencil

Approx 20in (50cm) Bondaweb

Fabric scraps in reds, pinks, oranges, and greens

Iron

Scissors

Selection of buttons

1. Turn the top of your pillowcase over by approximately 1½in (4cm) and press along the fold. Pin and sew along the line, leaving a gap at one side about 3in (8cm) long. You can use a sewing machine for this or stitch by hand using backstitch. Attach the safety pin to the end of the cord and feed into the top of your pillowcase through the gap you left. Tie the two ends together.

2. Use cookie cutters (or use the templates on page 123) to draw shapes onto the Bondaweb and draw some freehand leaves onto the Bondaweb as well.

3. Iron the Bondaweb shapes onto your scraps of fabric, following the manufacturer's instructions, and then cut around the shapes.

4. Arrange your flowers and leaves on the pillowcase. When you are happy with the arrangement, peel off the paper backing and iron onto the pillowcase, following the manufacturer's instructions.

fun fact

Most of the plants that we associate with Christmas, like the Christmas tree and holly and ivy, are European in origin and tradition, but did you know that the poinsettia is native to Mexico? Today it is known in Mexico as Noche Buena, which means Christmas Eve.

5. Choose buttons to go in the centers of each of the flowers and sew them on.

"You've Been Framed" Button Tree

NICARAGUA

For this project, we've used recycled buttons which are all in shades of green. If you have a collection of different colored buttons, you could make a Christmas bauble or the first letter of your name.

YOU WILL NEED

Templates on page 121

Pencil

Green card stock or paper

Scrap of gold paper

Scissors

Picture frame with glass removed—
ours was 8 x 12in (20 x 30cm)

White mat board (the same size as your frame)

Cutting mat

Craft knife

White glue (PVA)

Approx 50–60 green buttons in assorted sizes

Approx 5–10 red buttons
in assorted sizes

1. Trace the templates on page 121 onto paper and then use them to cut out a Christmas tree from green card and a star from gold paper.

2. Use the frame backing board as a template to cut a piece of white mat board to size, using a cutting mat and craft knife.

3. Place the mat board inside your frame and glue the Christmas tree and the star to the mat board. We positioned ours in the center of the frame.

4. Glue the green buttons onto the tree, trying to cover as much of the green paper as you can. You can glue buttons on top of each other too and don't be afraid to use a generous amount of glue. Glue the red buttons under the tree in a square shape to make the red bucket and then allow to dry flat for at least 24 hours.

Rockefeller Ice Queens

UNITED STATES OF AMERICA

When you hang these ice queens up they spin around as if they are twirling on ice. The trick is to use clear nylon thread so that they look as if they're magically spinning in the air!

YOU WILL NEED

Skater template on page 120

Black card

Pencil

Scissors

White card

Paper doilies (approx 6in/15cm diameter)

Glue stick

Small stick-on gems or pearls

Clear nylon thread

Embroidery needle

1. Trace or photocopy the template on page 120 onto black card to make a template that you can use again. Cut an ice skater out of white card.

2. Fold your doily in half. Find the center of the fold and cut a line measuring 1¼in (3cm) along the fold for the skirt's waist. Insert your ice skater through the hole.

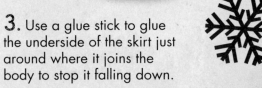

3. Use a glue stick to glue the underside of the skirt just around where it joins the body to stop it falling down.

4. Add your gems. We stuck them around our skater's neck, in her hair, and in a pattern on her skirt.

5. Thread a needle with nylon and push it through the bun at the top of the skater's head. Pull the thread until you are happy with the length and then trim and tie a knot.

fun fact

The ice rink at the Rockefeller Center in New York first opened on Christmas Day in 1956. It was originally built to draw customers to the high-end shops and restaurants but was so successful that it's become a permanent fixture.

Matchbox Manger

URUGUAY

When we were younger we would have regular competitions to see how many tiny things we could squeeze into a matchbox. Maybe you could squeeze in some other Christmassy things like a tiny star?

YOU WILL NEED

1 wooden bead, approx ⅝in (1.5cm) in diameter

Bamboo skewers

Pink, green, red, and brown acrylic paint

White pipe cleaner (chenille stem)

Scrap of white fabric

White glue (PVA)

Matchbox

Scrap of wood grain printed paper (we printed ours from the internet)

Scissors

Glue stick

Scraps of yarn, raffia, or paper

1. Stick your bead onto the end of a bamboo skewer to allow for easy painting. This will also ensure that the hole in the bead goes from top to bottom. Paint your bead pink and allow to dry.

2. Use another bamboo skewer to add eyes, mouth, cheeks, and hair with green, red, and brown acrylic paint. Allow to dry.

3. Push the pipe cleaner into the hole of the bead—it shouldn't come out of the top of the head. Fold the pipe cleaner over again and again until it measures roughly 1¼in (3cm). Twist it to make it a little more solid. This will be the body.

4. Wrap the white fabric scrap around the pipe cleaner and dab glue where the fabric crosses over to secure. Allow to dry.

5. Cut a piece of wood grain paper to fit around the matchbox sleeve. Glue on with a glue stick.

6. Cut some yarn, raffia, or paper to resemble straw and place inside the matchbox and then lay the baby on top.

fun fact

People in Uruguay celebrate Christmas by creating nativity scenes. Some families leave the manger empty until Christmas Day, when the baby Jesus is added.

Chapter 2

Europe

It's no surprise that the Christmas scenes we see on greetings cards and in books are usually from Europe, since many traditions come from there. Head over to Germany and make a Pay It Forward Advent Calendar, or try a pretty Stack It Up Christmas Tree, inspired by Estonia's claim to have had the very first Christmas tree!

Clothespin Christkind

AUSTRIA

This gorgeous girl looks complicated but with a little patience she'll come together in no time. A second pair of hands is useful too, when you're trying to put the clothespin into the pompom!

YOU WILL NEED

Heart template on page 120

Cereal packet or card

Scissors

Clothespin

Small matchbox, about 2 x 1⅜in (5 x 3.5cm)

Gold acrylic paint

Paintbrush

Black fine tip marker pen

Approx 14in (36cm) yellow yarn

Pompom template on page 120

Rainbow yarn

Approx 9in (23cm) florist's wire

16in (40cm) narrow red ribbon

Hot glue gun or strong glue

1. Use the heart template on page 120 to cut a small heart from card (you can use the card from a cereal packet). Paint the heart, clothespin, and matchbox with gold acrylic paint and allow to dry.

2. Using a black marker pen, draw eyes, a nose, and a mouth onto the clothespin.

3. Cut four 3-in (8-cm) lengths of yellow yarn. Spread some glue onto the top of the clothespin head and press on the wool. You may want to give her a little haircut at this point.

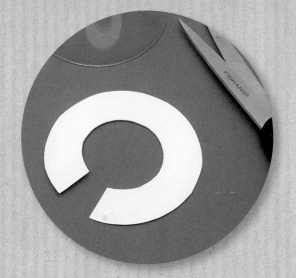

4. Using the pompom template on page 120, cut out two circles from your card or cereal packet. Cut out the gap at the bottom and the hole in the middle.

5. Hold the two templates together and start wrapping with rainbow yarn. Keep going until you have covered the card with three or four layers of yarn.

6. The next step is tricky and might be easier if you have two pairs of hands! Cut a piece of yarn 12in (30cm) long. Hold the pompom with one hand and cut through the two layers of card and the wool.

7. Gently tie the length of yarn around the middle of the pompom (between the two card circles) and at the same time insert your clothespin dolly. Tie tightly so that the dolly is in the center of the pompom. Remove the card and trim the tie.

8. Wind the piece of florist's wire twice around the dolly, just above the pompom. Bend wire arms about 1¼in (3cm) from each end and push into either end of the matchbox.

9. Tie the red ribbon around the box in a bow. Glue the heart on her back for wings and allow to dry.

fun fact

In Austria and many other areas of Europe and South America the traditional Christmas gift-giver is called the Christkind, which is German for Christ-child. The gift-giver is usually depicted as a child with blond hair and angel wings.

Glacial Lace Hangings

BELGIUM

These lace hanging decorations are a wonderful way to repurpose something unwanted into a beautiful Christmas decoration. You can pick up vintage doilies cheaply at secondhand stores. And because you're spraying the doilies, it doesn't matter if they're a bit yellow or old.

YOU WILL NEED

Lace doilies

Selection of embroidery hoops

Gold or silver enamel spray paint

Newspaper

Nylon thread or ribbon for hanging

1. Take one of your doilies and position centrally into an embroidery frame—make sure you choose one that fits into the frame while showing the lace pattern at its best.

2. Spray one side of the doily with paint—don't forget to protect your work surface with newspaper and work in a well-ventilated area. Allow to dry and then turn over and spray the other side. When the doily is fully dry, tie a piece of nylon thread or ribbon at the top of the hoop and hang it up.

fun fact

The city of Bruges in Belgium holds a Snow and Ice Sculpture Festival each year. Did you know that over 550 tons (500,000 kilos) of ice are used?

Cake Pop Cuties

CYPRUS

These gorgeous cake pops take a little longer to prepare than simple cakes or cookies, but are worth the extra time for their wow factor! You can substitute the decorations with anything else you might have in your store cupboard, or whatever takes your fancy in the supermarket!

YOU WILL NEED

1lb 2oz (500g) store-bought Christmas cake

2 bowls

Spoon

3½oz (100g) ready-made frosting (icing)

2¾ cups (500g) white chocolate melts or buttons

12–14 cake pop sticks or wooden skewers

Knife

Few sour straps candies, cut into thin strips

Tall glass jar to keep the cake pops upright until set

Mini rainbow chocolate chips

Handful of white mini marshmallows

1. Crumble the cake into a bowl until it looks like breadcrumbs. Mix in a spoonful or two of frosting (icing) until the mixture resembles a dough. Roll into balls—you'll need one for each body and a slightly smaller one for each head. Our bodies were about 1½in (4cm) in diameter and the heads were about 1¼in (3cm) in diameter.

2. Put the white chocolate into a separate bowl and ask an adult to help you to melt it in a microwave—you'll need to save a handful of buttons for the snowmen's hats. Dip the end of a cake pop stick into the chocolate. Slide the body onto the stick and then dip the stick into the chocolate again and add the head. Don't push the cake balls too far down—the head should sit at the top of the stick. Put the snowmen in the fridge for 10 minutes, or until the chocolate sets.

3. Remove the snowmen from the fridge and then dip each one in the melted chocolate using a rolling action. Gently tap your snowman against the side of the bowl to remove the excess chocolate (you may need to tidy up the base with a knife). Work quickly while the chocolate is still melted and then wrap a sour strap around his neck to make the scarf. Use a blunt knife to draw on a mouth in the chocolate. Stand each snowman upright in a glass jar to set.

4. Stick the mini chocolate chips onto the snowman for his face and buttons with a dab of chocolate or frosting. Finally, stick a chocolate button onto the top of the head with a bit of the melted chocolate and add a mini marshmallow on top to make the hat.

"Make a Scene" Terrarium

CZECH REPUBLIC

Terrariums can be made in any glass bowl or vase and provide a magical peek into a miniature world. You can make them for any occasion: try making an Easter terrarium with tiny fluffy chicks and Easter eggs.

YOU WILL NEED

FOR THE SNOWMAN

2 styrofoam balls, one 1in (2.5cm) in diameter and one ¾in (2cm) in diameter

Toothpick (cocktail stick), approx 2½in (6cm) long

Mini brads—in assorted colors

1 red button, ¾in (2cm) in diameter

3 red buttons, ⅜in (1cm) in diameter

White glue (PVA)

24in (60cm) red yarn

MAKING THE SNOWMAN

1. Thread the large and then the small styrofoam ball onto the toothpick.

2. Add two black brads for eyes, one orange brad for the nose, and three colored brads for buttons.

3. Glue your three smaller buttons together on top of the larger button in a stack to form the hat. When it is dry, secure to the top of the snowman's head with more glue. Cut the yarn into three equal lengths. Knot them together at one end and then braid (plait) them together to make a scarf. Tie a knot in the other end and then wind around your snowman's neck.

fun fact

Ice skating is very popular in the Czech Republic at Christmas time. Temporary ice skating rinks are set up in the capital, Prague, so that locals and tourists can show off their ice skating skills!

MAKING THE SKATER

1. Now make the skater. Cut the florist's wire into three lengths: 5in (12cm), 4in (10cm), and 3in (8cm). Form the 5in (12cm) piece into an oval and then twist the top together to form the neck. To make arms, find the middle of the 3in (8cm) length and, making sure you keep that in the center of the body, wrap each side around the wire of the body. For the legs, place the middle point of the 4in (10cm) length at the base of the body and then wrap each side around to secure.

2. To make the boots, cut a piece of fine jewelry wire measuring 2in (5cm). Thread it through one of the oval beads and wrap the end back under the bead to form the blade of the ice skate. Wind the other end up around the leg. Repeat on the other leg.

3. Cut the Q-tip in half and trim each half to 1in (2.5cm). Slide onto the ends of the arms. To dress your skater, start by winding yarn down one leg and back up it, then down the other leg and up again. Continue to wrap yarn up the skater's body and then around the arms and neck. Secure the ends with glue.

4. Push the styrofoam ball onto the neck. Cut equal lengths of yarn and glue onto the head to create hair. Add brads for eyes, if using, and use markers to draw a nose and mouth.

5. Wrap some more yarn around her neck for a scarf (you could also braid the yarn). Bend one of her legs up and ask an adult to help you to use a hot glue gun to attach her to the mirror.

ASSEMBLING THE TERRARIUM

1. Pour the shredded coconut into your jar. Tip the jar to one side so that you form a slope. Line up four of the matchsticks and glue a matchstick across them to make a fence. Allow to dry.

2. Bury the edge of your mirror with your skater attached into the shallow part of the coconut "snow." Add your trees, fence, and snowman, burying each of them slightly.

❄

YOU WILL NEED

TO ASSEMBLE THE TERRARIUM

Glass jar or vase, approx 10in (25cm) in diameter

6½ cups (500g) shredded (desiccated) coconut

5 matchsticks or craft sticks painted with green acrylic paint

Miniature trees

Underneath the Mistletoe Wreath

DENMARK

Curling and gluing paper makes a glorious, colorful three-dimensional wreath. We've used a hot glue gun for speed, but you could use white glue too, although the drying time will be longer and you'll need to hold the rosettes together with a paper clip.

YOU WILL NEED

30–40 squares of paper, 4 x 4in (10 x 10cm)—we used a mixture of plain and patterned scrapbook paper in reds and pinks

Pen

Scissors

Glue stick

Red card stock or paper, approx 12 x 12in (30 x 30cm)

Mat board, approx 12 x 12in (30 x 30cm)

Heart template on page 122

Pearl and crystal beads

Hot glue gun or white glue (PVA)

Scrap of green card stock or paper

12in (30cm) green ribbon

Red ribbon for hanging

1. Draw a rough spiral on each square of paper and cut out. You can try and cut out more than one at a time by cutting a few in a pile!

2. Starting in the center of the spiral, begin rolling it up into a rosette. Glue the end with a glue stick to secure. Glue your red card stock to the mat board using the glue stick.

3. Trace the template on page 122 onto paper. Fold a sheet of paper in half, position the half-heart template on the fold, and cut out. Open out the paper template and use it to cut out a heart shape from the card-covered mat board.

4. Ask an adult to help you use a hot glue gun to glue your rosettes to the heart, starting at one side and working your way around. Alternatively, use white glue. Glue a pearl or crystal bead in the center of each rosette.

fun fact

Did you know that woven paper hearts are a traditional Danish tree ornament? These beautiful red and white hearts have been made since the 1800s.

5. To make the mistletoe, cut eight teardrop shapes out of green card stock or paper. Fold your green ribbon in half and then glue four leaves to each ribbon end. Glue a few pearl beads for the berries, just above the leaves. Loop the green ribbon through the bottom of the wreath. Attach the red ribbon for hanging.

Stack it Up Christmas Trees

ESTONIA

These mini Christmas trees are a versatile little project. You can hang them on the tree or use one as a necklace. With the right jewelry making supplies (available in craft stores) you could also create a fabulous pair of earrings.

YOU WILL NEED

10–15 green buttons, ranging from ⅜–1¼in (1–3cm) in diameter

4 small red buttons, approx ⅜in (1cm) in diameter.

1 yellow star bead

8–24in (20–60cm) embroidery floss (thread) or baker's twine

White glue (PVA)

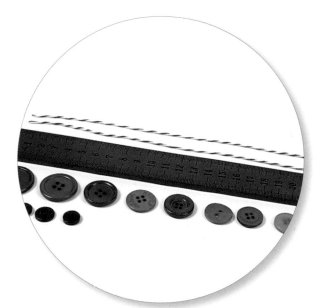

1. Select your green buttons and line them up from largest to smallest. Have your red buttons and yellow star bead to hand, too. Cut a piece of embroidery floss or baker's twine to the required length—24in (60cm) makes a necklace while 8in (20cm) would be a good length for a Christmas tree decoration.

2. Using your fingertips, rub a tiny amount of glue on the first ⅜in (1cm) of each end of the thread. This will stiffen it so that it doesn't unravel as you thread the buttons.

3. Push the thread up through both holes of the first red button. Make sure the button sits halfway and that both ends are even.

4. Repeat with the remaining buttons so that the two pieces of thread go up through each button. Start with the three remaining red buttons and then go from the largest green button to the smallest. Finally, add the yellow star bead. Knot the thread at the top with a simple overhand knot.

Color-in Christmas Cards

FINLAND

We used to make these little finger puppets with my mother when we were little — she'd cut out little teddy finger puppets for us to play with. She designed this sweet Santa finger puppet and we've put him in a card so this Christmas you can give a card and a present at the same time!

YOU WILL NEED

Templates on page 121

White card stock

Scissors

Felt-tip pens

Dark blue card stock

Glue stick

Stick-on diamanté gems

1. Photocopy the Santa and chimney templates on page 121 onto white card stock and cut them out. Cut another piece of white card stock to 6 x 8in (15 x 20cm) and fold to create a blank greeting card.

2. Color in your Santa and chimney using red, black, brown, and light brown felt-tip pens. Carefully cut out the finger holes in your Santa.

3. Cut two pieces of dark blue card stock, one measuring 4 x 6in (10 x 15cm) and one measuring 2 x 4in (5 x 10cm). Open your white card and use a glue stick to glue the larger piece of dark blue card stock onto the right-hand side. Glue three sides of the smaller piece and stick to the bottom of the card to make a pocket for your Santa puppet.

4. Stick the piece of card with the chimney on it to the front of the card. Use scissors to cut the front of the card just above the chimney until you get to the fold. Now cut down the fold, from the top of the card, to remove the top front of the card.

fun fact

Did you know that Santa has an official home town? He lives in Rovaniemi, which is the capital of Lapland in Finland.

5. Finally, pop the Santa puppet into the pocket and stick a few diamanté gems onto the dark blue background for snowballs.

65

Candy Cane Cookies

FRANCE

We need absolutely no encouragement to make a batch of these cookies! It's making them last long enough to decorate that's the tricky bit! The sanding sugar on these candy cane cookies adds a gorgeous texture — you'll be surprised how easy it is to make!

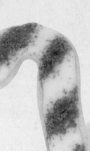

YOU WILL NEED

FOR THE DOUGH (WHICH MAKES ROUGHLY 40 COOKIES)

¾ cup (175g) softened butter

1 cup (200g) white sugar

2 eggs

½ tsp vanilla extract

2½ cups (250g) all-purpose (plain) flour

Nonstick parchment (baking) paper

Baking sheet

Rolling pin

Candy cane cookie cutter (or use the template on page 123)

Spatula

⅔ cup (125g) white sugar

Clean glass jar with lid

Red food coloring

2 cups (250g) confectioner's (icing) sugar

Knife

Stripe template on page 123, photocopied onto thick paper

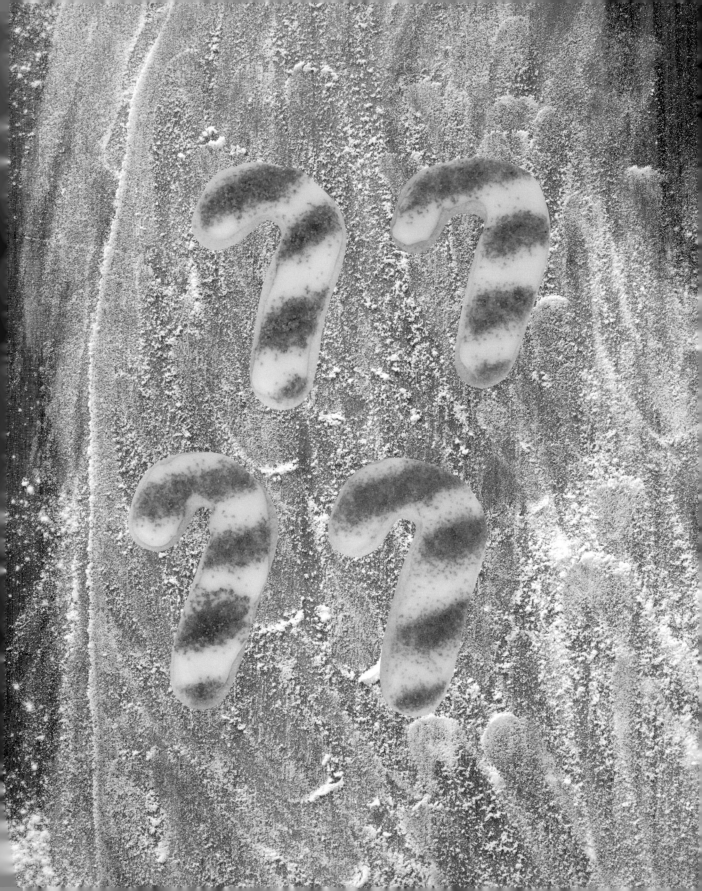

1. Preheat the oven to 400°F (200°C/Gas 6). Line a baking sheet with nonstick parchment paper. Place all the dough ingredients into an electric food mixer fitted with a dough hook and mix until a dough forms. If you don't have an electric mixer, cream the butter and sugar together and then beat in the eggs and vanilla. Finally, add the flour and mix until a dough forms. Place in the fridge to chill for 5–10 minutes.

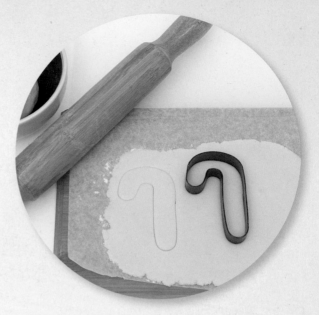

2. Roll out your cookie dough to about ¼in (6mm) between two sheets of nonstick parchment paper. Cut out your candy cane shapes and transfer them to the baking sheet. Bake in the preheated oven for 7–8 minutes or until golden and then transfer to a wire rack to cool with a spatula.

3. Put the sugar in your glass jar and add 10 drops of red food coloring.

4. Add the lid and shake the sugar until all the color is mixed. Pour into a bowl.

5. Put the confectioner's (icing) sugar into a bowl and add water, a little at a time, until you have a smooth, spreadable icing. Ice the first cookie with a knife.

6. Hold the stripe template over the iced cookie. You'll need to work fairly quickly so that the icing doesn't dry. Sprinkle the red sanding sugar through the template onto the iced cookie. Gently tap the cookie to remove excess sugar and then allow to harden. Repeat with the other cookies. Any leftover red sugar can be stored and reused for another time.

fun fact

Did you know that bredele or bredala are biscuits or small cakes, traditionally baked at Christmas in the Alsace region of France? There are lots of different varieties of bredele.

Pay It Forward Advent Calendar

GERMANY

We love a chocolate Advent calendar as much as the next person. But we were thinking, wouldn't it be good to give something back in the days leading up to Christmas, instead of taking? You can make up your own list of actions. Think about simple gestures, such as smiling, or holding open a door for someone!

1

10

9

YOU WILL NEED

Templates on page 124

Pencil and pens

Laminating sheets and laminator (optional)

White card stock (optional)

Glue stick

Scissors

Craft pegs or clothespins

Hot glue gun or strong glue

Assorted scrapbook paper

Assorted card stock

Red ribbon, approx ¼in (6mm) wide

Single hole punch

Baker's twine

1. Photocopy the scallop shape template on page 124—you'll need 25. Write the numbers 1–25 on each one and then laminate and cut out. If you are not going to laminate the numbers, you'll need to glue them onto a thicker card stock and then cut them out.

2. Ask an adult to help you use a hot glue gun to glue each number onto a craft peg or clothespin. Alternatively use strong glue.

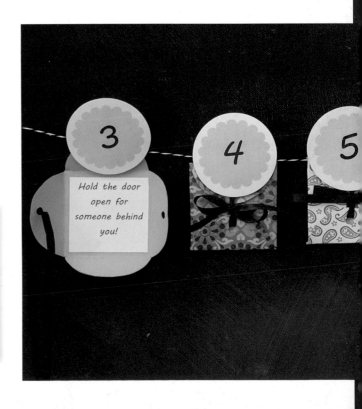

Hold the door open for someone behind you!

fun fact

Did you know that the first Advent calendars were made in Germany in the 1800s? Before this, Advent was marked by the lighting of candles or by drawing chalk lines on doors.

3. Photocopy the envelope template on page 124 and cut out. Use a glue stick to stick together pieces of scrapbook paper (we used Christmas themed paper) and colored card stock until you have enough sheets to cut out 25 envelope shapes.

4. Type or write up a list of actions on white paper—stick to simple things that you will be able to achieve, such as "Give someone a hug" or "Bake someone some cookies." Cut each one out and stick in the center of each envelope, on the card stock side. Fold each of the four flaps in.

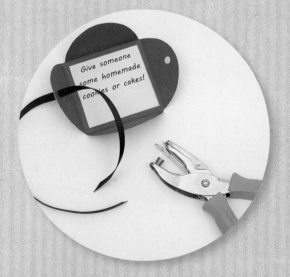

5. Use the hole punch to punch a hole on two of the facing round edges. Cut 25 pieces of ribbon, each 12in (30cm) long, thread through the two holes and tie into a bow.

6. Take a long length of baker's twine and use the number "clips" to attach the envelopes. Your Advent calendar is ready to hang up!

Quick Make Panettone Plate

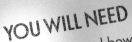

ITALY

Cakes look lovely on an elegant cake stand but these are often way out of our price range. Use ceramic or strong glue to make a stand at home, using budget or thrifted crockery. We bought inexpensive matching bowls and a plate, but you could experiment with vintage finds. Why not use a glass vase or sundae glass as a stand instead of the bowls?

YOU WILL NEED
2 matching cereal bowls
1 dinner plate
Ceramic or strong glue

NOTE
Clean this cake plate by wiping it with a damp cloth—we don't recommend putting it in the dishwasher.

1. Make sure your bowls are clean and dry. Turn one bowl upside down and run a line of glue around the bottom rim of the bowl. Take the second bowl and put it the right way up on top of the first bowl. Press down lightly and then leave to set (check the instructions on the glue).

2. Run a line of glue around the rim of the top bowl and position the dinner plate on top. Press down lightly and then let it set.

fun fact

Panettone is a sweet bread that originally comes from Milan in Italy. Did you know that it is one of the symbols of Milan? Today it is eaten as a Christmas food all around the world.

Heart Felt Tree Charm

POLAND

These pretty little decorations can be made by the tiniest of fingers. If younger children find it too hard to push the needle through several layers of felt, they could just use one layer.

YOU WILL NEED

Assorted felt pieces

A set of heart-shaped cookie cutters (or use the templates on page 124)

A set of round cookie cutters (optional)

Pen

Scissors

Embroidery floss (thread)

Embroidery needle

1. Use either your cookie cutters or the templates on page 124 to draw three heart shapes in different sizes from three different felt colors. You could also use round cookie cutters to make round tree charms.

3. Cut a piece of thread 8in (20cm) long and thread onto your needle. Push the needle through the top of the heart in the center and pull halfway through. Make sure the threads are even, knot at the top, and hang on your tree!

2. Layer the three hearts on top of each other and secure them together by stitching a cross in the center. To do this, first knot your thread. Put the needle in through the center of your hearts, from back to front, and then out to each corner of the cross and back to the center each time. Knot at the back when finished and trim the thread.

fun fact

In Poland, a special Advent activity is baking gingerbread, which is called pierniczki. Pierniczki are made in lots of shapes, including hearts and animals.

Tea Light Table Twinklers

RUSSIA

These little candle holders use cheap tea light candles and old glass jars, so all you'll need to splash out on are the glass paints — but even then you might be able to find bargains in your local craft store.

YOU WILL NEED

3 clean and dry glass jars

Glass paints in yellow, red, and green

Paintbrush

Paper and pen

Gold glass outliner or paint

Tea light candles

1. Paint your jars. We built up the color by painting one coat, leaving it to dry, and then painting another coat.

2. Sketch out a few designs on paper until you are happy with your design. Then use your gold outliner paint to draw the designs on your jars. We did a basic tree, baubles, and snowflakes. Allow to dry, according to the manufacturer's instructions. Put a tea light candle in each jar and light the candles! Never leave a burning candle unattended.

fun fact

Did you know that Russians have New Year trees instead of Christmas trees? Traditionally, tree ornaments were made of glass, cotton, card, or wire.

Cookie Cutter Clay Decorations

SWEDEN

Using cookie cutters to cut shapes out of clay gives a lovely crisp outline. These clay decorations have all the charm of ginger biscuits, but once you've made them, they'll last forever!

YOU WILL NEED

Package of quick-drying clay

Rolling pin

Christmas cookie cutters—we used an angel, tree, and reindeer

Pencil

Acrylic paints

Paintbrushes

Colored and patterned ribbons

1. Roll out the clay on a flat surface as if you were rolling out cookie dough until it is about ⅛in (3mm) thick. Using the cookie cutters, cut out your shapes.

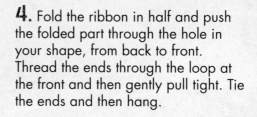

2. Make a hole at the top with a pencil or small paintbrush. Make sure your hole is big enough to push the ribbon through. Let dry. This could take 24 hours, so allow plenty of time. The warmer the room, the quicker the drying time.

3. Paint the top of the shapes, let dry, and then turn over and paint the other side. Acrylic paint is quick-drying so you won't need to wait long for it to dry.

4. Fold the ribbon in half and push the folded part through the hole in your shape, from back to front. Thread the ends through the loop at the front and then gently pull tight. Tie the ends and then hang.

fun fact

In Norway and Sweden, it is traditional to make ginger cookies called pepparkakor with your children at Christmas. If they are to be used as window decorations, then they are rolled a little thicker than usual and decorated.

Turkish Delightful Cupcakes

TURKEY

This Turkish delight cupcake is a showstopper designed by our friends at Buttercrème Lane Bakery in Sydney. We've made one cupcake with the full tree as the centerpiece and then decorated the remainder more simply. These would make a really pretty Christmas afternoon tea.

YOU WILL NEED

12 plain cupcakes
(these can be homemade
or store-bought)

½ x 16oz (450g)
tub of ready-made vanilla
frosting (icing)

3½oz (100g) Turkish delight

Silver dragées (balls)
or sugar pearls

1. Use a knife to spread each cupcake with the ready-made frosting. Then chop the Turkish delight into rough cubes, approximately ¾in (2cm).

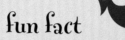

fun fact

Turkish delight is a delicious soft dessert from Turkey, which is often eaten as a treat around the world at Christmas. The most common flavors are rosewater, orange, and lemon.

2. Start stacking the Turkish delight cubes on the cupcake. Build one layer and add dabs of frosting as you go to hold it together. Make it narrower as you go up, like a Christmas tree.

3. Add silver dragées to decorate your tree using dabs of frosting to hold them in place. Decorate the remaining cakes with silver dragées. Enjoy!

Berry Special
Napkin Rings and Runner

UNITED KINGDOM

One of the best parts of any celebration is the preparation — dressing a table for a Christmas meal really builds the excitement! Imagine how thrilled your guests will be when they find out that you have handmade the napkin rings and runner?

YOU WILL NEED
(FOR 1 TABLE RUNNER AND 1 NAPKIN RING)

Berry templates on page 125

2 sheets of red felt

2 sheets of green felt

Scissors and pen

Sewing machine and sewing thread

Single strand silver sequin trimming, ¼in (6mm) wide

White glue (PVA)

2 red bells, 1¼in (3cm) in diameter

11in (27cm) red ribbon, ¾in (2cm) wide

MAKING THE TABLE RUNNER

1. Using the templates on page 125, cut out 15 berries from red felt and six large and two small holly leaves from green felt (the small ones are for your napkin ring).

2. Use your sewing machine to sew the berries and leaves together in a long line by machine stitching through the center of each felt piece and feeding the next piece through the sewing machine when you get to the end. We did a pattern of one leaf and then three berries but you could do a random design.

3. Cut lengths of sequin strands to fit the length of your leaves. Run a line of white glue along the stitching on the leaves and then stick your sequin strands onto each leaf.

MAKING THE NAPKIN RING

1. Take the two small holly leaves that you cut earlier, fold in half and cut a slit down the center of each one about ¾in (2cm) long. You should have a slit that is 1½in (4cm) long when unfolded.

2. Tie a small red bell onto each end of the red ribbon. Gently feed the bells through both leaves to secure.

fun fact

The United Kingdom is made up of England, Wales, Scotland, and Northern Ireland. "The Holly and The Ivy" is a traditional English Christmas carol and holly has been used to celebrate Christmas since the 15th century. Did you know that in large quantities, holly berries are poisonous?

Chapter 3

Asia, Africa, and Oceania

These regions generally see warmer weather than the chilly white Christmases we associate with the holiday. That said, Christmas traditions are just as big here as they are around the world. Why not spread some Aussie Christmas sunshine with our Bondi Beach Baubles, or make a delightfully jingly Ethiopian Sistrum Stick to play on Christmas Day?

Bondi Beach Baubles

AUSTRALIA

These beach ball Christmas tree decorations will bring a slice of Australia to your home! It's a great project for using up tiny scraps of bright fabrics and the white glue gives them a subtle shine. You might not be near a sunny beach on Christmas Day but you'll be able to share this little patch of sunshine with your friends!

YOU WILL NEED

Fabric scraps in bright colors
Template on page 122
Scissors
Styrofoam ball, 2½in (6cm) in diameter
Screw eye
White glue (PVA)
Glue brush
Ric rac trim or ribbon
8in (20cm) ribbon, for hanging

1. Photocopy the template on page 122 and use it to cut eight pieces of fabric in different colors.

2. Screw the eye into the Styrofoam ball—this will help you hold onto your ball while you cover it with fabric. Paint glue onto the ball, stick your first piece of fabric on, and then paint glue over the top. You may want to let the glue dry halfway round to make it easier to handle. Continue until you have covered the ball with all eight pieces.

3. Cut a length of ric rac trim or ribbon to go around the ball—it should be about 8in (20cm) long. Glue the ball first, then stick the ribbon down and glue over the top. Allow to dry.

fun fact

Christmas in Australia is hot and summery, which is the opposite of the snowy Christmas images used in Europe. Many Europeans who now live in Australia celebrate Christmas in July, when the weather feels more Christmassy and cold!

4. Thread the hanging ribbon through the screw eye at the top of the bauble and tie a knot in the ends. Now hang on your tree!

Quick Paper Quilt

CHINA

Make this wall quilt as small or as large as you like! You can also vary the piece sizes. We've used a "tesselating" triangle — this is an equilateral triangle, which makes it easier to create a mosaic pattern, but you could experiment with a more complicated shape or shapes. The best bit about this project is that it is quick to put up... and equally quick to take down. It also takes up very little room to store for next year!

YOU WILL NEED

Several sheets of sparkly card stock, in assorted colors

Triangle template on page 122

Pencil

Scissors or craft knife, ruler, and cutting mat

Adhesive tack, such as Blu Tack®

Spirit level (optional)

1. Our star is made up of 108 triangles. You can make yours smaller or larger to fit your wall space. Trace around the template on page 122 and use it to cut out your triangles. You can use scissors, or a craft knife, ruler, and a cutting mat.

2. Use a small amount of adhesive tack in the top half of each triangle and press to the wall. We used a spirit level to check our triangles stayed straight. Arrange your triangles until you're happy with the colors and shape. Our star shape has three upright triangles at the base of each point, so once you have created the first point, the rest is easy! We also left a little space between triangles, which allows for less than perfect cutting. Stand back and admire!

fun fact

Hong Kong is a part of China, situated on China's south coast. In Hong Kong, it is traditional to decorate Christmas trees with chains, flowers, and lanterns, all made from paper.

Santa Sistrum Stick

The jingle bells we've used in this project make a lovely sleigh-bell sound, so that when you shake your stick you'll be immediately transported to Christmas night!

ETHIOPIA

YOU WILL NEED

A wooden spoon

Acrylic paints

Paintbrush

Black marker pen

5 jingle bells, approx ⅝in (1.5cm) in diameter

20in (50cm) ribbon

1. Paint an oval face shape on the spoon. We mixed a little red paint with white to make pink but you can use any skin color you like. Allow to dry. Paint on Santa's hat and two red cheeks. Allow to dry and then draw on Santa's face with a black marker pen.

2. Add Santa's white beard and the pompom on his hat, using white paint.

3. Thread each bell onto the the ribbon and push them along to the center of the ribbon. Tie the ribbon around the handle of the spoon. We wrapped it around twice and then tied a bow.

fun fact

In January, Ethiopians celebrate the baptism of Jesus with a festival called Timkat. During the Timkat procession, musical instruments like the sistrum stick are played. The sistrum stick looks a bit like a vertical tambourine.

Shine Bright Fairy Lights

INDIA

Christmas just wouldn't be Christmas without a string — or several strings — of fairy lights. Draped on the tree or anywhere else inside or outside the house, these tiny lights look great on their own, but even better with a little decoration! We used scrapbook paper to make our stars but you could experiment with shiny or glittery paper if you wanted to add even more sparkle!

YOU WILL NEED

String of fairy lights

6 sheets of card stock (3 red, 3 green)

Christmas scrapbook paper

Glue stick

Star-shaped cookie cutter, approx 2in (5cm) across

Pencil

Scissors

Single hole punch

Sticky tape (optional)

1. Glue pieces of scrapbook paper to your card stock, so that it is patterned on one side and plain on the other.

2. Use the cookie cutter to draw stars onto the card stock—you'll need one star for each light. Cut out each star.

3. Punch a hole in the center of each star and then cut a slit across to this hole.

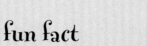

fun fact

People celebrating Christmas in India hang beautiful, huge, star-shaped paper lanterns outside homes and shops.

4. Slip a star over each light until all the lights on your string have a star. You may need to put a piece of sticky tape on the card to secure them in place.

We Three Washi Window Clings

IRAN

Washi tape is a versatile and easy to use craft material that we seem to be addicted to! You can adapt this project for any occasion — how about a window display of hearts on Valentine's Day, or some sweet pumpkins at Halloween?

YOU WILL NEED

Crown templates on page 126

Thin card

Pencil

Scissors

Sticky back plastic

Assorted washi tape

1. Transfer the templates on page 126 onto thin card, then cut around them and use them to draw crown shapes onto the paper side of the sticky back plastic.

2. Flip the sticky back plastic over and cover the shape you have just drawn with strips of washi tape. Our lines of washi tape were neatly joined together but you could overlap them or leave spaces. Flip the sticky back plastic back over and cut out the shapes around your template line.

3. Now they are ready to stick on your window! Peel off the paper backing but keep it somewhere safe so that when you remove your window clings you can store them to use again!

"Oh My!" Origami Gift Box

JAPAN

Paper gift boxes can be expensive, so why not make a few of these and fill them with small presents? You can change the size of the template on a photocopier to make larger boxes, if you prefer.

YOU WILL NEED

Templates on page 126

Pencil

Thin card

Scissors

2 pieces of green scrapbook paper—we used Christmas themed paper

Small piece of red paper or card stock

Glue stick

2. Using the template as a guide, fold along the dashed lines. The half lines near the wavy edge need to be cut with scissors. Fold into a box shape and glue the tabs.

1. Glue two pieces of green scrapbook paper together. Transfer the template on page 126 onto thin card and use it to cut the box template out of the scrapbook paper. Use the berry template to cut two berry shapes from red paper or card stock.

3. Fold the rounded flaps in and then slot the holly leaves together.

4. Slide the berries together into the slits on either side of the holly. Now you can fill your beautiful box!

Starry Starry Night Lantern

PHILIPPINES

We've given you a list of the materials for the lantern we made, but you can use whatever you can find. Maybe you'd like to use patterned ribbons or narrow strips of fabric? Sequin strips would sparkle in the light beautifully!

YOU WILL NEED

3 egg cartons

Scissors

Gold acrylic paint

Paintbrush

Hot glue gun

12in (30cm) paper lantern

Star gem stickers

Assorted ribbons and braids

32in (80cm) yellow embroidery floss (thread)

Approx 20 crystal beads

Assorted feathers

Nylon thread

String of battery-operated fairy lights

1. First make your gold stars, so they have time to dry. Cut the cones out of the inside of the egg cartons. Paint each cone with gold acrylic paint, inside and out. Allow to dry.

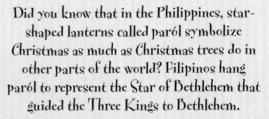

2. Snip all the way around your cones almost to the point. Ask an adult to help you use a hot glue gun to glue two cones together, one inside the other, and gently splay out. Glue onto the lantern. We started at the top of the lantern and glued our stars in a line going down to the bottom. Add some glittery star gems around the stars.

3. Cut all of your ribbons and braids into 32in (80cm) lengths. Thread 20 crystal beads onto a piece of embroidery floss (thread).

4. Tie the ribbons and braids onto the bottom of the lantern by folding each one in half and placing it one side of the wire at the bottom of the lantern. Feed the two ends of the ribbon or braid through the loop that you have made and pull gently to tighten. Tie the embroidery floss onto the wire. Repeat with more ribbon and braid until you're happy with how it looks. You can vary the lengths if you like. Glue feathers onto the ends of some of the ribbons and tie a piece of nylon thread at the top for hanging. Fill the lantern with fairy lights, turn on, and hang up.

fun fact

Did you know that in the Philippines, star-shaped lanterns called paról symbolize Christmas as much as Christmas trees do in other parts of the world? Filipinos hang paról to represent the Star of Bethlehem that guided the Three Kings to Bethlehem.

Hark The Herald Hat

SOUTH AFRICA

My father would make these little angels each year at Christmas with his math classes. He would make his pupils work out the various measurements so the end result would be a sweet surprise! Here, we've taken the hard work out of them and given you a template to draw around. That way you can whip up as many as you like for your Christmas guests!

YOU WILL NEED

Patterned gift wrap

Card stock

Glue stick

Template on page 124

Scissors

Single hole punch

12in (30cm) narrow elastic, approx ⅛in (3mm) wide

1. Glue a piece of gift wrap to a piece of card stock. We used a Christmassy red. Allow to dry.

2. Copy the template on page 124 onto a piece of paper and lie it on top of the card stock. Cut around it and then cut through all the black lines, through both layers.

3. Slot lines A and B together to form the angel. Punch two holes, either side of the hat, and tie the elastic onto one side. Adjust the length of the elastic to fit around your head and tie to the other side.

Snowball Fight Pompoms

SOUTH KOREA

Pompoms can be made from any material, providing you can wind and cut it. Using this t-shirt fabric gives the pompom a great chunky texture and would make them super soft in a pretend snowball fight!

YOU WILL NEED

Cereal packet or card

Bowl approx 5in (12cm) in diameter and glass approx 2¾in (7cm) in diameter, or use the template on page 120

Pen

Scissors

White t-shirt or tank top

1yd (1m) baker's twine

White glue (PVA)

Iridescent white glitter

2 bowls or plates

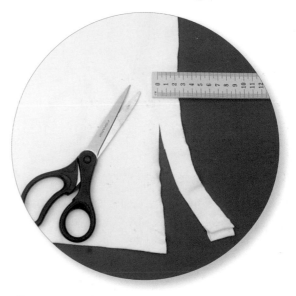

1. Draw around the bowl and glass onto a cereal packet to make a pompom template, or copy the template on page 120, and cut out two card circles. Cut out the inner circles.

2. Cut the t-shirt into strips approximately ¾in (2cm) wide by cutting along the bottom of the t-shirt. Snip one side of each strip so that you have several long lengths.

3. Wind your t-shirt strips around the pompom card circles until you have covered it with three or four layers of fabric.

4. Cut through the layers of fabric, between the two card discs.

fun fact

Did you know that South Korea is a top winter tourist destination? While the ski season runs from November through March, a good time to visit is in January when hundreds of thousands of Koreans visit the Hwacheon region for its Sancheoneo Ice Festival. This festival features a Winter City Plaza of ice sculptures, rides on a traditional Korean sled, and ice fishing.

6. Pour PVA glue into one bowl and glitter into another. Dip the pompom into the glue until it coats the ends of the fabric all round. Dip into the glitter, shake off the excess, and let the glue dry before hanging.

5. Wrap the baker's twine between the card discs and tie it tightly.

"Stitch 'Em Up" Christmas Trees

YOU WILL NEED

8 sheets of Christmas scrapbook paper

Glue stick

Template on page 125

Card stock

Pencil

Scissors

Sewing machine and sewing thread

THAILAND

These little Christmas trees make a sweet table centerpiece but they can also be made into gorgeous tree decorations! Simply leave a longer thread at the top of the tree to tie them on. Sewing together simple circles will give you Christmas baubles, too!

1. Glue your scrapbook paper together to make four double-sided sheets.

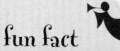
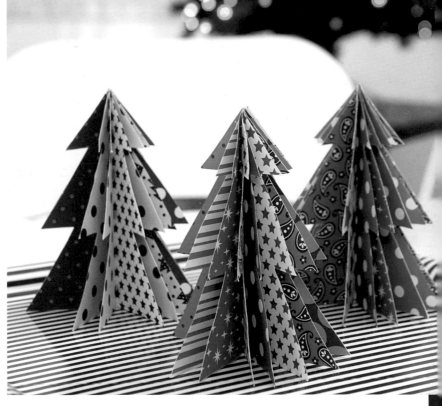

2. Transfer the Christmas tree template on page 125 to a piece of card stock and cut it out. Use the template to cut eight tree shapes from the double-sided paper.

3. Stack the eight trees together in a pile and sew a straight line from the bottom of the tree to the top. Snip off the loose threads—leave a thread at the top if you want to hang as a tree decoration. Fold the "branches" to fan out the tree and stand up. These look great in little groups, so make as many as you like!

Beautiful Button Bowl

ZAMBIA

Button bowls can be a bit fiddly to make but the reward is a glossy, colorful bowl that will be a gorgeous Christmas centerpiece for your table. Keep to a couple of colors, or use a random assortment for a rainbow bowl!

YOU WILL NEED
Large shallow bowl

Plastic wrap (cling film)

White glue (PVA)

Paintbrush

An assortment of buttons of all sizes

NOTE

This bowl is not food safe and cannot be immersed in water or put in the dishwasher. Use it to display pinecones, wrapped lollipops and candies, or other Christmas treats.

1. Cover the inside of your bowl with a layer of plastic wrap (cling film). It may help to spray some oil onto the bowl first so that the wrap sticks.

2. Paint a generous layer of white glue onto the plastic wrap in your bowl shape.

3. Working from the center of the bowl outward, lay your buttons flat in the bowl. Try and place the buttons as close together as you can. Keep going until you get to the size you want and think about whether you want a straight or wavy edge. Let the bowl dry—this could take overnight.

4. Paint another layer of glue over the top of the buttons to seal the bowl. Make sure you get plenty of glue in the spaces between the buttons. Let the bowl dry for at least 12 hours. Gently remove the button bowl from the bowl mold, peel off the plastic wrap, and allow to thoroughly dry. Trim any excess dried glue until you are happy with the shape.

fun fact

Every year across Africa everyday objects are recycled into beautiful gifts and given around the world.

Glossary

ACRYLIC PAINT
A water-soluble paint that you can use on many different surfaces like paper, canvas, and wood. It can be difficult to get out of clothing when it dries.

ADHESIVE TACK (BLU TACK®)
A reusable putty-like temporary adhesive.

AIR-DRYING CLAY
Clay that dries hard in the air without the need for a kiln or oven.

BAKER'S TWINE
Soft cotton yarn, often with two colors spun together, such as white and red.

BAMBOO SKEWERS
Thin bamboo sticks used in cooking. Available in supermarkets.

BONDAWEB
Bondaweb is a paper-backed, iron-on transfer adhesive. It permanently bonds fabrics together quickly and easily. It is ideal for appliqué.

BRADS
Decorative split pins. Available from stores where you can buy scrapbooking supplies.

BUTCHER'S PAPER
Large sheets or rolls of cheap paper, often used in packing.

CAKE POP STICKS
Plastic or paper sticks made specifically for making cake pops. Available in craft or cake decorating stores.

CARD STOCK
Thicker than paper but thinner than mat board.

CORD
Cord is a rope-like yarn made by twisting or plying two or more strands of yarn together.

CORK MAT
Round cork mats are often sold as pot stands or coasters. Available at home wares stores and supermarkets.

CRAFT STICKS
Flat wooden sticks that look like popsicle or lolly sticks.

CUTTING MAT AND CRAFT KNIFE
Ideal for cutting card stock or mat board, or when you want a really straight line. A self-healing mat protects your table or work surface. The safest craft knives have retractable blades. They should be used with adult supervision.

DIAMANTÉS
A small ornament that looks like a diamond or gem.

DOLLY CLOTHESPINS
Old-fashioned wooden clothespins (clothes pegs), now more commonly used for craft projects than for hanging out laundry.

DOWEL
Cylindrical wooden rod in various diameters and lengths. Available from craft or hardware stores.

EMBROIDERY FLOSS (THREAD)
Embroidery floss or embroidery thread is thicker than machine thread but thinner than yarn. It is used for hand embroidery.

EMBROIDERY HOOP
Two hoops of bamboo or plastic that fit together, trapping a piece of fabric. They are used to keep fabric tight and flat when you are working embroidery.

EMBROIDERY NEEDLE
Embroidery needles come in a variety of sizes. Look for one with an eye that will fit your embroidery floss (thread).

ENAMEL SPRAY PAINT
Enamel spray paint in an aerosol can.

FELT
Non-woven cloth made by matting fibers together. Traditionally made of wool, craft felt is now more often made from synthetic fibers.

FELT BALLS
Made by dipping wool fibers into hot soapy water and rolling into a ball until the fibers felt together.

FLORIST'S WIRE
Comes in a variety of colors and sizes. Used for flower arranging and other art and craft projects.

FOOD DYE
Liquid or powder dye used in food.

GLASS PAINT
A paint made specifically for painting glass. Other paints won't adhere to the shiny surface.

ACRYLIC PAINT

BRADS

EMBROIDERY HOOP

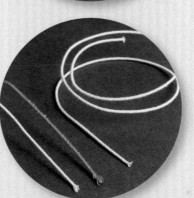

FLORIST'S WIRE

GLUE GUN
Electric tool which melts hot glue gun sticks to provide a glue with a strong bond.

GLUE STICK
Solid glue in a twist-up tube suitable for paper and card crafts.

IRIDESCENT GLITTER
Iridescent glitter appears to change color as you look at it.

JEWELRY WIRE
Fine wire used in jewelry making.

JINGLE BELLS
Small decorative bells. Available in craft stores.

LACE DOILIES
Ornamental lace mats.

LAMINATOR AND LAMINATING SHEETS
A machine that uses heat to seal paper between two layers of thin plastic sheet.

MAT BOARD
A type of cardboard, usually with a color on one side and white on the other. It is used for mounting artwork in a frame.

MDF COASTER
Round flat piece of MDF, ideal for embellishment and available at craft stores.

NYLON THREAD
Strong clear nylon thread often used in beading. You could substitute it for fishing line. Also available as stretchy nylon thread which is used to make bracelets, etc.

PAPER DOILIES
Decorative paper punched with a lace-like pattern used in food presentation and craft. Available at craft stores and supermarkets.

PARCHMENT/BAKING PAPER
Paper resistant to grease or oil that is used in cooking. Available from supermarkets.

PERMANENT PEN
Pen with permanent ink.

PINKING SHEARS
Scissors with zigzag blades. They are used to stop fabric fraying or to add a decorative edge.

PIPE CLEANER
Also known as a chenille stem. They are colored polyester fibers on a wire stem.

POMPOMS
Pompoms are decorative balls usually made from yarn or fabric.

PVA
White glue that can be cleaned up or diluted with water. It can also be painted onto craft items to give a glossy finish.

Q-TIPS OR COTTON BUDS
Cotton-ended sticks.

RIC RAC TRIM
A flat narrow braid woven in zigzag form, used as a fabric trimming for craft, clothing, and upholstery.

SCRAPBOOK PAPER
Printed paper available in beautiful designs. You can buy it in single sheets, or in books at craft stores.

SCREW EYE
A screw eye has a screw thread at one end and a ring at the other. Available at craft and hardware stores.

SELF-ADHESIVE CHALKBOARD VINYL
Easy-to-use chalkboard with adhesive backing. Can be cut to any size and stuck on a flat surface.

SHREDDED (DESICCATED) COCONUT
Dried and shredded flakes of coconut.

SINGLE STRAND SEQUIN TRIM
Sequins that come sewn together in a continuous line.

SOFT SUGAR PEARLS OR BALLS
Cake decoration available from cake decorating suppliers or supermarkets.

SPIRIT LEVEL
A tool designed to indicate whether a surface is perfectly horizontal or vertical.

SPONGE PAINTBRUSH
A sponge paintbrush has a piece of sponge in place of bristles. You can use them for glue, varnish, or paint.

SPRAY VARNISH
Easy-to-use varnish that comes in an aerosol can. When using, make sure you ventilate the area well to avoid the fumes.

STICKY BACK PLASTIC
Clear plastic on a roll with one adhesive side.

STRONG GLUE
Solvent-based glue, stronger than white or PVA glue—for example UHU.

STYROFOAM BALL
Lightweight craft material available in various shapes and sizes.

TISSUE PAPER
Lightweight paper available in a huge variety of colors.

WASHI TAPE
Decorative paper masking tape that originated in Japan. Available in a huge range of designs, from craft stores.

WATER-BASED MARKERS
Washable pens used in art and craft.

WIRE CUTTERS
A specific tool used for cutting through wire.

YARN
Yarn can be made from natural and synthetic fibers. It can be used for various crafts, including knitting and crochet.

PINKING SHEARS

WASHI TAPE

Templates

All the templates except "Oh My!" Origami Gift Box (Japan) are provided at full size, so you just need to trace them off the page.

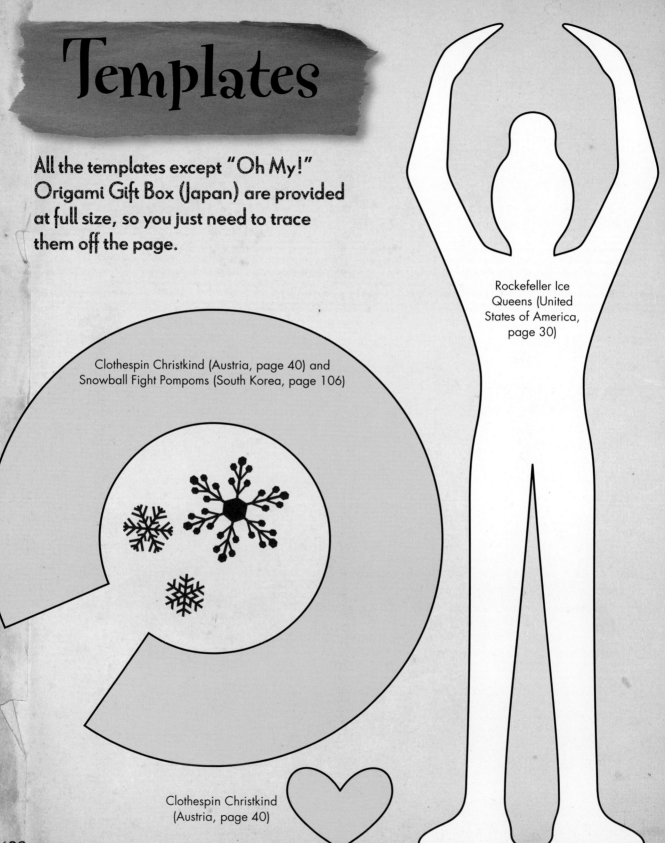

Rockefeller Ice Queens (United States of America, page 30)

Clothespin Christkind (Austria, page 40) and Snowball Fight Pompoms (South Korea, page 106)

Clothespin Christkind (Austria, page 40)

"You've Been Framed" Button Tree
(Nicaragua, page 26)

Color-in Christmas Cards
(Finland, page 62)

Color-in Christmas Cards (Finland, page 62)

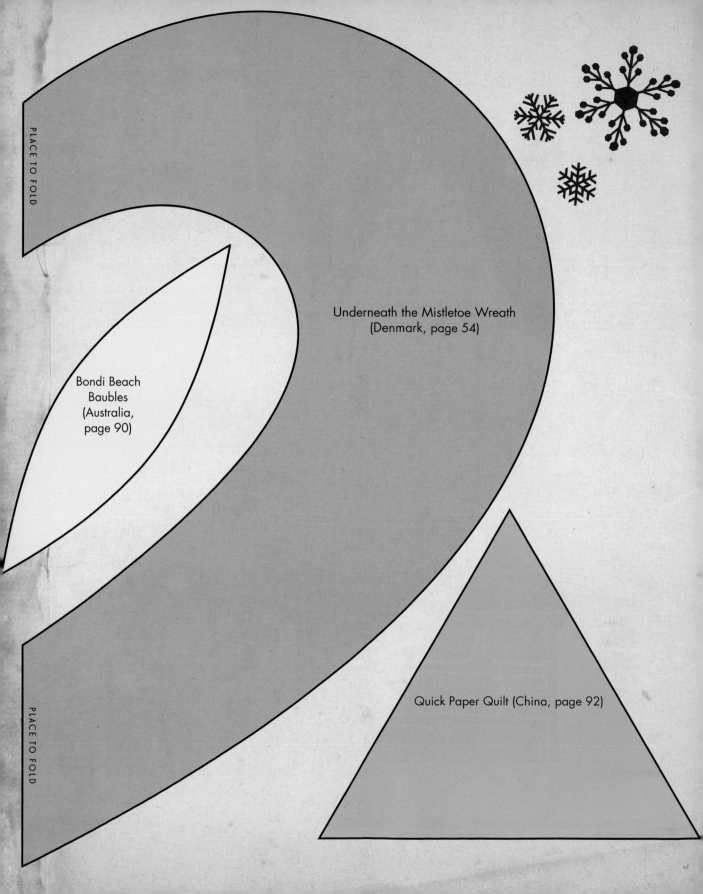

PLACE TO FOLD

Underneath the Mistletoe Wreath
(Denmark, page 54)

Bondi Beach
Baubles
(Australia,
page 90)

PLACE TO FOLD

Quick Paper Quilt (China, page 92)

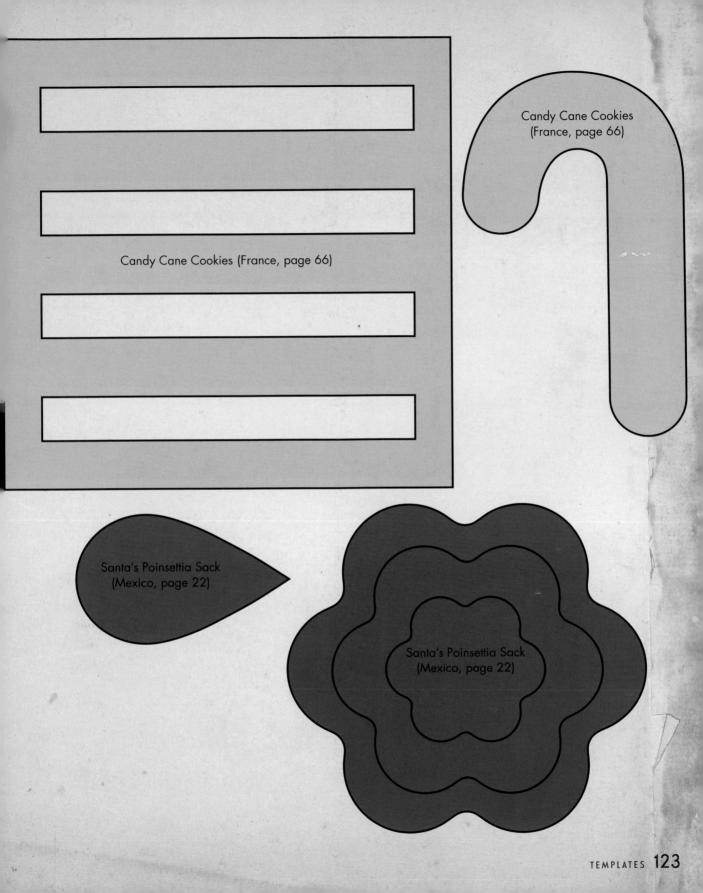

Candy Cane Cookies (France, page 66)

Candy Cane Cookies
(France, page 66)

Santa's Poinsettia Sack
(Mexico, page 22)

Santa's Poinsettia Sack
(Mexico, page 22)

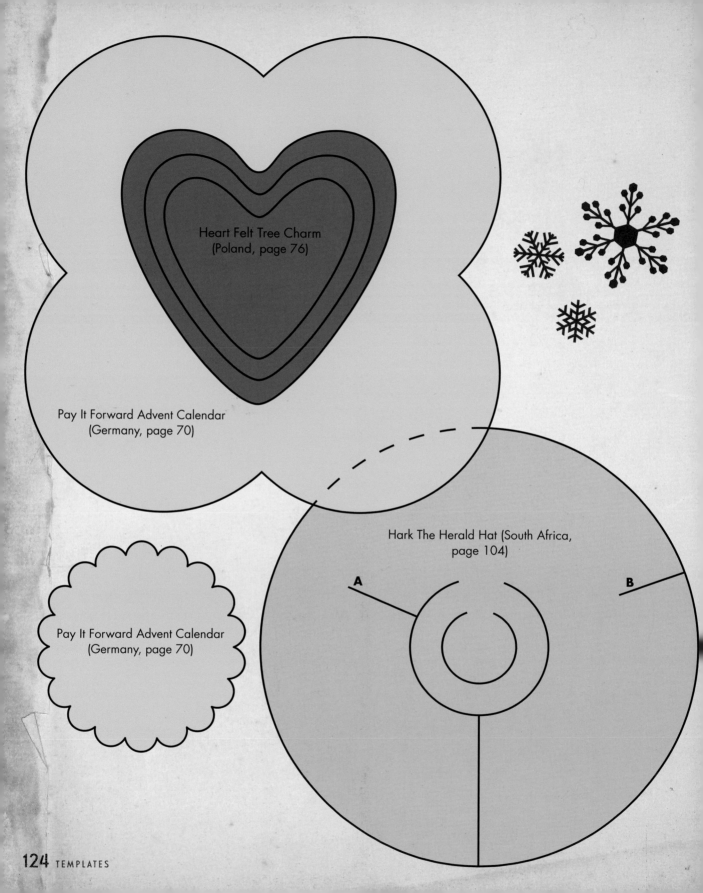

Heart Felt Tree Charm
(Poland, page 76)

Pay It Forward Advent Calendar
(Germany, page 70)

Pay It Forward Advent Calendar
(Germany, page 70)

Hark The Herald Hat (South Africa,
page 104)

A

B

"Stitch 'Em Up" Christmas Trees
(Thailand, page 110)

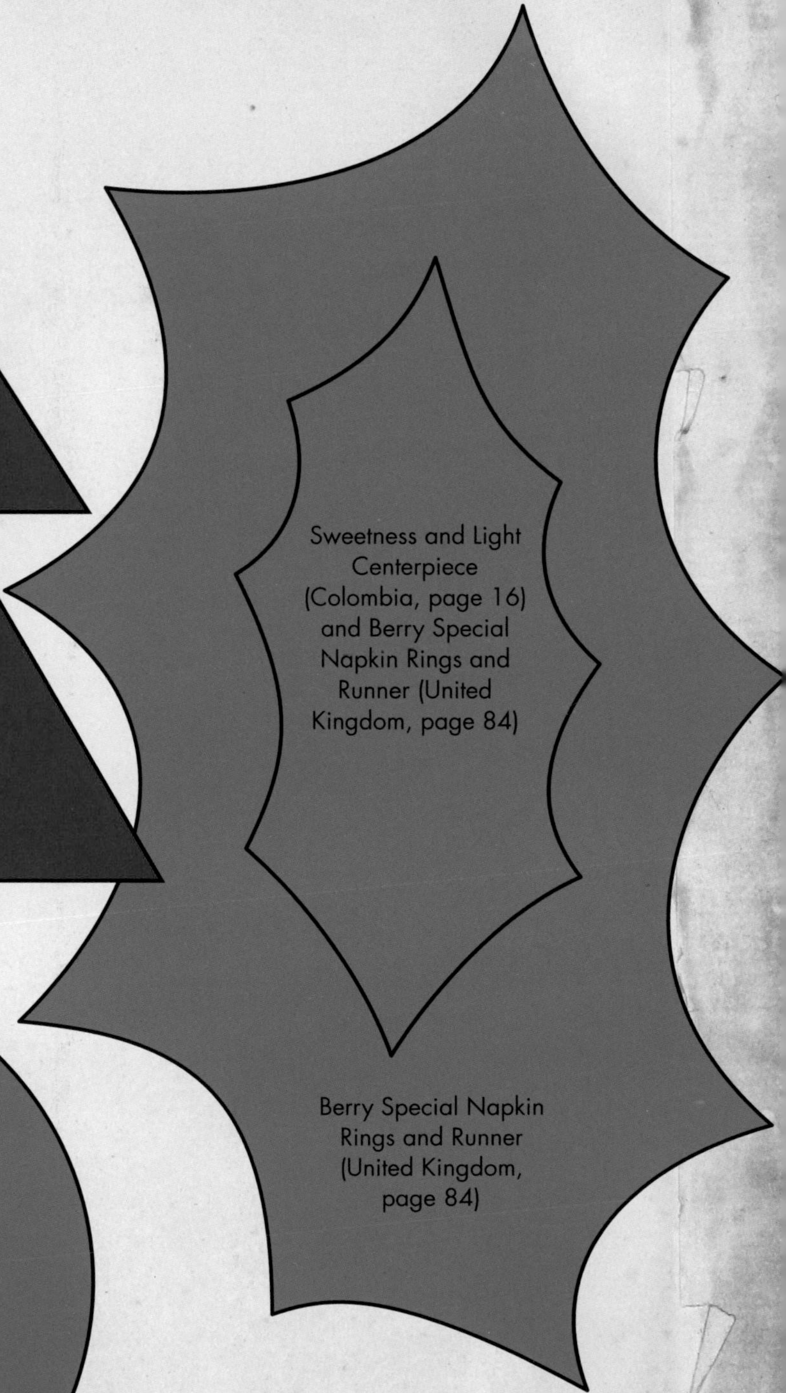

Sweetness and Light
Centerpiece
(Colombia, page 16)
and Berry Special
Napkin Rings and
Runner (United
Kingdom, page 84)

Berry Special Napkin
Rings and Runner
(United Kingdom,
page 84)

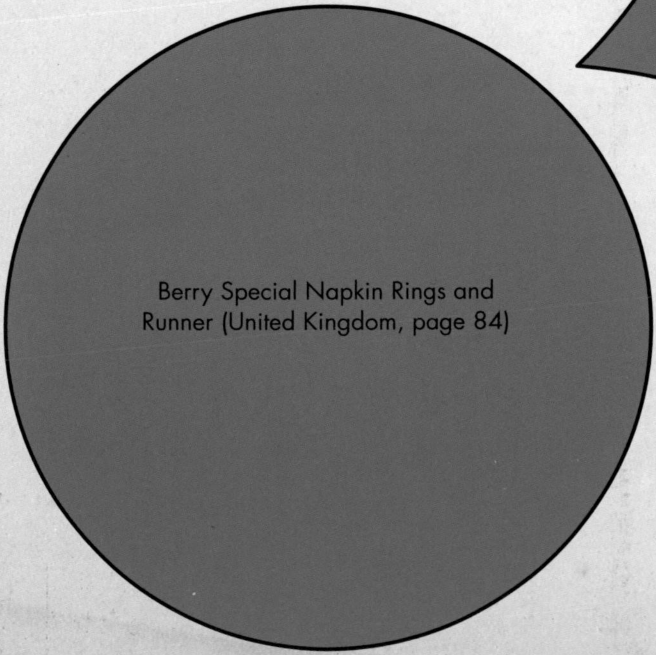

Berry Special Napkin Rings and
Runner (United Kingdom, page 84)

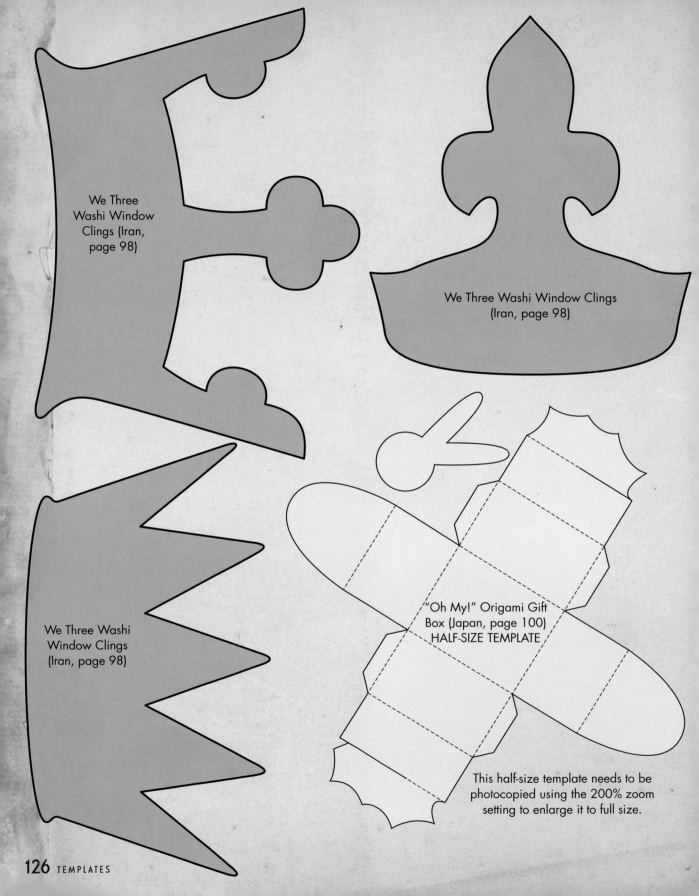

We Three Washi Window Clings (Iran, page 98)

We Three Washi Window Clings (Iran, page 98)

We Three Washi Window Clings (Iran, page 98)

"Oh My!" Origami Gift Box (Japan, page 100) HALF-SIZE TEMPLATE

This half-size template needs to be photocopied using the 200% zoom setting to enlarge it to full size.

Suppliers

AUSTRALIA

Buttercrème Lane
www.buttercremelane.com.au

Bunnings Warehouse
www.bunnings.com.au

Cleverpatch
www.cleverpatch.com.au

Eckersley's Arts and Crafts
www.eckersleys.com.au

Lincraft
www.lincraft.com.au

Riot
www.riotstores.com.au

Spotlight
www.spotlight.com.au
*Supplier of "Prints Charming"
fabrics, which are used in this book*

Typo
shop.cottonon.com/shop/typo

US

A C Moore
www.acmoore.com

Create for Less
www.createforless.com

Darice
www.darice.com

Hobby Lobby
www.hobbylobby.com

**Jo-Ann Fabric
and Craft Stores**
www.joann.com

Michaels
www.michaels.com

UK

Baker Ross
www.bakerross.co.uk

Homecrafts Direct
www.homecrafts.co.uk

Hobbycraft
www.hobbycraft.co.uk

John Lewis
www.johnlewis.com

M is for make
www.misformake.co.uk

Yellow Moon
www.yellowmoon.org.uk

Index

Acknowledgments

Thanks once again to Cindy Richards and Carmel
Edmonds. Love as always to our parents, Ross and
Sandra and Pat and Jon, and our siblings,
Amanda, Ben, Jane, and Susan. Thank you to the
brilliant Daniella Boutros from Buttercrème Lane
Bakery in Sydney for her inspired cupcake design.
Libby would like to thank Cath Derksema from Prints
Charming for her friendship and guidance. Thanks
to Samantha Hainsworth for her unwavering
support and wine. And a special acknowledgment
of Rebecca Larratt. A star who shone brightly but
for too short a time. Starry Starry Night is
dedicated to you.